Gallery Books
*Editor* Peter Fallon

MY LOVE HAS FARED INLAND

Medbh McGuckian

# MY LOVE HAS FARED INLAND

Gallery Books

*My Love Has Fared Inland*
is first published
simultaneously in paperback
and in a clothbound edition
on 30 September 2008.

The Gallery Press
Loughcrew
Oldcastle
County Meath
Ireland

www.gallerypress.com

ISBN 978 1 85235 452 7 *paperback*
       978 1 85235 453 4 *clothbound*

A CIP catalogue record for this book
is available from the British Library.

# Contents

*for Ruth and Marcus Kennedy*

*It is when sound abandons the servile function of signification, and develops itself freely as music, that it becomes thoroughly vital and its own excuse for being.*

— George Santayana

## Painting by Moonlight

It was a bright inviting, freely formed,
though I suppose it was I who brightened,
with an internal scattering of light,
as though weather maps were more real
than the breath of autumn.

The low colourfulness
of the broken and dying leaves
was no embrittlement
to every decided colour on the sunlighted grass
and the warm-hued wood of his door.

But with the dust descending
in the glaring white gap
my backbone pulped and I closed up
like a concertina.

His tongue was hushed as Christ's lips
or once-red grapes permitting
each touch to spread only
when the turn of the violet comes.

## Painting a Verb Half Golden

The horizon is in danger,
just off the real land grown on.
Thoughts rub against it and it aches
like a poisonous otherworldly
black star.

The wind blows between it
and the steep face of the wave
that changes the way my fingers
are and the feel of the lines
of my skin.

When blue was nothing
I let you turn my wrist white
and scorch my tongue to living silver
with your young gold:
I let a pretty red hold

me like salt on its side,
and when I was alone
blue's opposite
left a naked grey
at the corner of my eye.

The coats of my eye
like a red-blue couple
recycle your shadow, mortal as words,
blue lying on the rose,
an inverted blue tree:

and next to your mouth,
though the rain does not paint softly,
the deepest pen-shaped groove
would be deliberately too light
for wine-press or pine-cone . . .

## Duncairn Balanda

One should not pay pearl-price
for old velvets, or the chair which assists
the work of the skeleton, the scalloped mirror
basking in lustre after sunset.

Many doorbells had been out of order
for years. Despite the sold-off triangle
of land the gardens continued to be taxed
by the lucky owners of shoes.

A grey trembling flame left the ceilings
in profound darkness which gave them
a patriotic look, as if they were peppered
with handwritten letters, or fingers

seemed to walk across the breast.
Wrinkles in the elbow called memories
slept in our daytime clothes.
When the two ships were made fast

together, in a grotesque bouquet,
having twice changed the name
on her bow and stern, they started up
car engines to muffle the sounds to come.

A happy music during sad occasions.

When they poured perfume into their eyes,
and also ate snow, she healed their skin
with potato leaves and sugar,
hugging the fact that this was her house.

## The Nailflower

There are no paths where they are moving,
the whispering man with his blue heart,
and full-body halo of spiky juniper:
the woman made only of water and earth
who shields herself with her prayer book —

a cinnamon demureness, down the mannered
length of her arm, and one hand resting
on the other's wrist like five outsize pearls.
Her neckline no lower than centimetres,
a silk even more sheer starts at midbreast,

each temple waiting for its feast day.
He tucks a nailflower into her olive belt
and, though the daytime sky is not yet overdark,
the twenty-seven minutes of music
through which their death is passing

seem a ten-day season to the more common
Christian angels in this orphaned painting:
even the last movement of the eyes
once the mirrors have been placed there
is nuptial-shaped as a triangle of sea.

## The Gold that is Worn by God

The star or crown that an angel
once drew in the snow
is either not shown or trimmed away:

this lack of desire for snow
as what winter should be
I place around my wrist for safe keeping.

A skintight coat of mail.
And since it is said one does not age
in the time spent regarding the Host

will these false rains
of a pilgrim season
become voices again

in differing fields,
pressed against the back
of a god-coloured valley,

like a bed of white bronze
looking out through the rent
in a strawberry?

## Carving Colour

I smoothed it too soon,
the fading has been absolute.
But it is more than its completeness,
larger against the sea as we have it here.

I polished a cruel material
to show its grain, stone shape
and no other shape, giving the wayward
creases an ennobling, classical skin.

My hand asleep and fully matter
is also a listening hand, my everyday tongue
recalls chains of words like pale blue
genuflecting holes

where autumn leaves have come to rest
firmly on the embroidery. The fox
is now a blue ghostly patch
on the soul of the forest,

as if a year's worth
of earth-coloured light
were breaking through the features
at its seemingly lowest points.

# Sealed Composition

*One learns only from those one loves.*

— Goethe

It is a little like returning to life,
with a new spinal cord that reddens your throat,
your untended name, dreaming and probing,
seeing and testing the consolation
of new gospels.

The cloaked girl, all-too-human sharer
of his flaming tomb,
is flower-reading the transfigured
anti-city, lecturing on mercy, a lady
of the mind, his mind's moated bride.

The seraph's second wing
reverses the needle of happiness
at the wrist, a pilot-angel,
an epiphany in black anxiety,
he snaps his helmet shut on his face.

The slowest of heavens, going up
and down another's stairway,
smothers their angelic ivory boat
in cold and intimate brown tones:
their dry lips find themselves on the reached shore.

## Unsound Ship

I grew so stony, so polished within,
I was constantly taking closed flowers away,
trying to gather my life into a single
act of vigil remote from praise.

I have never dared glimpse your night-time spine,
your heavy, soothed body high
in my dreams, or held you as if for sale
everywhere I want you to be.

My pupil would be stunned
by the cold weight of your breath,
your everquietness, your minimum of folds,
your source of coolness turned into gold.

There is dependable rain
paving your dubious roads and, more
illusory still, an hour when light
of all kinds plays upon it,

while air with its superior intelligence
passes by on love's way with a pleasing
lightness of foot; and time, foreign to our
planet, pungent as it was, has been bloated

without a beyond — as if in hospital
at the height of summer the bits
and pieces of evening have fallen
to the appetite's sandy floor.

# *The Serin*

St Barbara, patroness of miners,
is your protector, from the All Saints' flood.
You are the ghost of too-young love
at either end of a century
combing fields for apples,
living off blackberries.

You look around and reach
over-the-shoulder piercing glances
to initiate night-nesting,
a silver-backed furnace
like black bread or a horse potato
wrapped in straw.

Farm beneath sand, desert curling
in the ocean, ice-fair on the river,
your hazy red and yellow snowflakes
flaring every fourth winter day
encrust the sea-salted windows of the city
with the tremor of brown and flesh-coloured

down-welling snow. In the Julys
you are a cool and grey summer
named after an uknown polar flower.
When the tongue of the glacier is very thin
one can see the chapel door
through the weakened ice;

and, at rogation-tide,
read afresh
its effaced fresco,
under modern sun,
of the straits of St Bonifacio
you once lived near.

## Bashali

I feel he would give it to me in spirit
as rivers carve out kingdoms,
the boulder field near the watermill,
my father's summer land.

He would give it in my children's
father's name, a crucial terrain
anchored and perturbed,
for thinking in spring about fall

and in summer about the purest time
of winter. If this clothed throat
like a nowhere-to-be-found pool
that shelters under the youngest mountain

could be seen the new breaths
of three hundred dark roses'
third day would tell it all,
holding a door in your arms.

## The Snow Crab

It was a fragrant December. Satin-voiced.
The earth launched from its anchor hold,
in many lungs all at once
turned vertically the shape of a mouth.

Showings of the host-like moon
flickered between book and door,
most present when about to be lost,
semi-lunar, fringed and watching.

Her head was held by four different hands,
four coffins perfectly nested,
tied with nine silk ribbons
that rubbed charcoal into small cuts

and, on one knee, a cross.
Downwind, only a narrow shelf
of membrane circled his eyes
in black, like smaller baskets

full of earth, with a spill
of oil rich in water:
the bee returning from a nuptial flight
emitting his floral odour.

## The Realm of Nothing Whatever

The difference between things
that are really the same is called
Three in the Morning.

The pigeon's bath and the tiger's regard,
the dawn air and the night air,
bird-stretchings and bear-hangings
and pillowed corpse on corpse.

The broken tile sunk
in the wide house
with the desolate side windows
that zero summer,

the pearl forever irritating the oyster
with inexorable tenderness,

the small earth cannot just file past
the bracing flood-breath of another planet
as if nothing has happened.

You do well to fade away
as if at a border crossing,
fashioning your vanishing
to end without force
in a minimum, rocking note.

# The Bird Calendar

I never thought of them together
so close to other boats,
this creasing at the wrist of a sunburnt
male arm drawing her hand
in its unfinished sleeve,
with this brown-gold crouching Venus
shown with her mouth bound
over a valance of shot greens and mauves.

Each time I came back crushed
by the swept-back curtain, the gold
thread in her silk hair-bag
that once had a narrower fall,
the graceful cascade of sheets
from a *notte*, a night-scene,
marked by his opalescent touch,
the elegant pink slipper he has signed.

Only years separate them within,
like the faraway red on a childbirth tray,
an April setting in the winter of words,
the abandoned plough which signals autumn.
I listen to the streets breathe a second,
hundreds of miles of new streets
breathing a saffron scent of make-believe
countryside and warmer buildings,

and call it his Japan, his view of the road,
a more untouched road piercing the forest,
reconciled to the river as a cushion
for the bridge, the leap of its comforting
arches: call this slim luxurious window
the garden as a happy refuge
or a site for danger, this squarish leaf
a sharply defined, glistening tree

by the principle of glittering
and the assumption of enough blue
to give the feel of air to the blue
enflowered cathedral rougher than the russet
of a poor twisted Christ of the twelfth century —
simplified, in the moist outdoor imitation,
evidence of a sky, a simple blue sky,
at the lighted edge of the wall.

## The Inferno Machine

If everything has its angel,
if everyone entrusted with a certain mission
is called 'an angel',
what makes heaven in a person?

A tailored fragrance,
a glistening altar,
for cherries a finger placed
under one people-watching eye?

That evening of electro-melancholy,
yours were the happiest eyes,
a mirror from the 1960s
and the old black houses.

Your skin responding to the slightest
touch, clear as a bell,
suggested grapes picked while frozen,
the way the land lies,

so smooth, girded with plaited
willow. My violas of humility
would have brought you marzipan
as you lay dying,

or a ninety-nine bead rosary
of organic silver from Japan,
as if you were Mary yourself.
But your active, must-have wings

were mellow lounging scrap gold
on the light-coloured stone
of the night stair.
In the fragrance library

of the angel trees
the wings of time were broken
and hooves were knotted at his throat:
the river now less than half

its winter height.

## Starrinarosa

A moment when the garden has emptied
and spring is seen from the inside,
in its partition; the designer has worked
peach and silver into the deep red
behind the white acts.

An oddly courtly moment,
almost as if one frayed marriage
were pressed into a single board,
and both were blinded
by one long breath,

talking while dancing,
taking movement risks,
her face churned in the travel time
of his hand and arm: her shoulder
turned every colour of the rainbow.

Still her spine is straight, so far they kneel,
she bounces her wrists together
to make that lily by sheer will,
needs to fold her knees perfectly,
lean against parts of her nakedness.

The male side of the bed
lies down on the female side,
ices it, then kisses it, with no
continuous touching, watches the landed
kiss cure everything,

even (as time would have it)
this thousand-year-long, evening-length hour,
far from sunny; the expectant,
bell-like star-costume
crushed ill-scented into the ground.

## The Human Ladders

Everything today
in the rain-soaked garden looked neglected;
at a forbidden part of the garden
an apron fully carved with death,

with a coffin road and a kinless ghost
a boat-grave and otherworldly sounds.
To finish the death I poured water
over the entire body,

over its gold and silver bridges,
a libation to the spirit of the sea.
Was the bitterness burnished and polished
like a heart-protecting mirror

above its own kneeler, bearing
the continuance of brushing
instead of truly counting
from roost to roost until lost?

The treed yard allowed
other sounds, post-dawn,
the crown of the song tree
sent branches dead as bread

crashing to the forest floor.
With or without nests,
the built world tracks
the dark-handed image of your hand,

the moulding of your lips'
reversed blossoms plucked

labially. The young parts
of vines spread out to sleep,

semi-evergreen, a garnish
of mid-ribs of leaves
and overwide grasses.
They sleep draped over the rim

of the tree bowl
and the day nest,
of the sleeping tree
and the herb nest,

they hang in outstretched
star postures, grippingly,
from the fruitless tree
and the death tree,

raindrops and dewdrops
sieved in the palm
of the bemirrored
room.

## The Book Moth

To feel as though I were still master
of the days, this evening
I took up my Dante *Companion* again,
and a moth stored deep within the senses
flew as a final shock
from behind the warm bookcase.

As one who cannot even turn
in his bed without assistance,
I saw him go down the narrow room
that made the whole house so unbearably
thin, withdrawn from eternity
for so short a time.

I was tempted to kiss his death-mask,
his lip-rebellion, his single eyelash, the tautness
of his skin which only virgins have,
the glass-eyed harvest of that decisive look
whereby the everyday world
appears to be saved.

But I closed the door behind him
like a pair of hands held in pockets
or a fair of mourning at a graveside,
repeating once more that nothing
remains to be said, to re-cut
the inscription on my mother's tombstone.

The head and breast of the dead woman
were in the foreground, the breast
with its imperfections tangential
to the altar — slipping cloths
and glasses in disarray —
the atmosphere of lamps almost at night.

A dark-haired servant woman
with blue at the back of her neck
and a less forgiving blackness
between them down below.
My own blacks were pushed too far,
my whites not far enough

to photograph in the twilight
the grey garden, the carefully swallowed
streets. When colours stubbornly
take positions that they no longer leave
they divide something local
that has never been divided,

like the flexibility of the throat
or half-tones on horses' backs,
the shine on a painting of the Only
lying halfway between the sheen
and the earnest moonlight
caught serenading the New Year.

## Eleven-bead Rosary

He could not sleep, would not step
back. Looking out of second-storey
windows at our fields, which wash themselves
with soil, his skin remembered
landscapes sedimented in her
that her body welcomed,
the withheld, silk-tongued rains
that stormed her island by island
till their incense sealed her off
from the path of rain itself.

Then the winds switched direction
as if it was daylight, stiffened as if
to sabotage a harvest with their stolen
melodies and demands. He would consecrate
one night of the week, burning his mind
to the spirit spouse he carved and fed,
her wooden self on second contact
copied by his own inner arrow,
a wooden rifle turning bullets to water,
circuiting the town removed from the map.

# The Cliff of Thought of Renunciation

Slight colour from the weak, late-night sunlight,
lesser reds, like a barely broken dawn.
The ship is like leaf at the island's ceramic rim,
moths circle the net of the wild courtyard.

As it wishes, spring fragrance may cease,
summer-lidded mountains, clearing autumn skies,
an inkling of winter and golden snow
sprout four seasons, all in one sitting room.

Desire steps in, a poorwill entering the door,
his inch-wide pupils resting repeatedly
on the forest geometry of the tray landscape,
his eyes the eyes of a mountain.

He presents his throat like a cherrystone
carved in a hundred facets, the lyrebird
shape of his ear, the fruits and vegetables
that make up the river diary of his head.

And complete in his breast, within him,
a cloud-dream-lake, a cloud-terrace
ladder of spaces, where we sleep together
in the windswept glimmer of shrine lamps.

## Solar-powered Garden

The first garden was small and gently sloped
to echo the house. The second reads
as a black spill to which the greys
of the sky are fitted.

Grey garden now, in the angle
of the weakening moonlight,
beginning to lose its shape,
its backbone awaits the spade

like a four-hundred-year-old meadow
or all-over fields on a cliff edge
leading your eye to a rose-arch
or a nut walk where windbreaks

and double late summer borders
paint out the weed-like traits
with a touch — no more — of red:
a chosen petal from one frozen

satinflower tasting what the weather
rediscovers and tells,
as though the blue in the sky
could be one thing.

## The Snowflake Album

Black and grey walkers,
each bird watches the wave approaching
its neared end, its bounded sounds.

Every bird makes the same decision
at the same time, whether
the marsh water
could really be paler,
or more untidy,

if sun and shade are equally
divided on the grass.

In the shaded light of our houses
the snowflake's branching lies flat,
in spite of the angel's advice
to view such emotions as are seasonal
with the tulip's innocent alertness.

The work of the sapphire
is called shining and spoken
by the self-sustaining lightness
of the male deity of day:

those rays which to themselves are all eye.

## At the Angel Concert

An accurate mirror is held to the flower.
The lace-clad bed is undraped by its first dream.
The eyes of death may be so swiftly trained.

Your clear-edged body sees in far-off snow
how you went instinctively to the window,
your ringless hand invisible inside your coat,

using one hand to imprison the excuse
of your other hand's loudest pulse
spared by the fire in its silken grip.

There are diamonds re-reading your collarbone:
robes that stood piquantly as a hedge
away from your body settle richly

around your lower body's shifting hem.
They train your spine when to release
the teased hair that lets your face

brim with a momentary meaning,
that would not ever be a muse of fire
melting into blackness on a Swedish river.

# Broca's Area

*for the centenary of the birth of Patrick Kavanagh*

How well one can hear the mind of a book
on an east sea road, the gold in sea-water!
Though the water in the lake is quite old
I rediscover dawn and twilight here
as the sea lily experiences the heliopause
of a warm moon paler than grass
that causes the coiled tongue of the frog to unfurl:
Echo, that nymph of words without meaning,
was triply beautiful to this reader of dreams
and gentle drugs; she fevered the orphaned
muscles of his lame hand to a marker
for storminess, while black-clad women snow-choked
his separate ice-tongue with their haggard faces.
But he also went out by the slaughterhouses.

## Shot Angel

A gentle pink, close to pain,
was making the sky follow
the innards of the landscape.

The sun's intense amber
slipped a near-human warmth
over the handleless door

so that it seemed to clip
and hinge together
in a fan of blue zigzags

like the rowlock of a gondola.
I could see, starting as though
from a cloud, the child's green aura,

the very essence of his head
deep-sheltered in the open curves
of the blankets, his split and drilled

face. And a field with dark edges
in the fusion of his mouth and ear.
One might question the absence of roads,

the funnelling paths
crisscrossed with narrow tracks,
and the stylized spires

in some lesser stone
at the hushed heart of his map.
No map, however exquisite,

can ever show everything,
the wind cherubs tinted
just the red a woman's lips should be.

## The Sin Eater

Angel of the Agony, I have found
no name for you yet. I am trying
to fix the sounds, but am I really
alone in this unadorned music?

Their long sleeps threw them into
an elbow chair sweetened with my blood,
like a best-selling funeral sermon
or when those seasons are separated from you.

Kneeling down after three steps,
walking backwards all the way,
I heard a military Mass play,
and worked my trust in God into the floor.

Which step was the real death
on the nicely polished marble,
the wild, old-fashioned, secret death,
the oldest death there is?

I closed my eyes with my own fingers
but further opened my haloed body,
the swerves of fantasy docked
in the isthmus of my neck

till the lavender-flowered garden
was more scented
than if I had been blessed
with a fragrant wife.

## Sidereum Iter (His Journey through the Stars)

Something about every pebble
in front of the hall door
is a soft boundary easily crossed
to the elegance of the leaf copper grasses
as high as a horse's bridle
and the unaltered crystals
at the beryl blue mouth of the glen.

The tower fabric of these enigmatic
buildings, their semi-engaged
turrets projecting outwards
and their windows ascending clockwise
like a low skyline church,
sets a barrier against the fall of night
at all fifteen river mouths
right around our shores.

As a sign of health
he was shown the sun moving backwards
over ten lines on the sundial,
so that the day was almost
doubled in length.

Nor was there night nor even dusk
in that province for the following twelve
nights while they celebrated his passing.
The evening star did not bring
in its dark wing the star-bearing shadows.
The people of the Ulaidh tell
that till the end of that year
the nights were not so long
as they had been.

Like maps backed in blue silk,
the sky's colour fell between

the two most intense shades
in that ensemble of all the high peaks:
he would not find himself in hermit
country, moss campion, the highest
flowering plant, two butterflies
above the snout of the glacier.

## Watching the Owls with You

Only two people are allowed in the room,
a room designed to imprison,
from the dark inside, in the Arab air,
its door wound and closed.

An almost empty coffin,
as if the earth refused to take
what remained, he died indeed
just like the least important human being,

so gently and so quickly!
If your richness were shared with me,
oh churchyard, this extinct
flightless bird that sleeps

twenty hours a day,
this erect, headless spirit
with its hands and feet bound behind,
mystified in time,

would line the exit
with the continued miracle
of his own play-being, no better,
just as I have burned these threads

and they will not come back:
just like a bringing-back,
just as these names are cold,
the names of the horses

and the names of the angels
place the world as a somewhere
deep in this circle of the sky.
But what she knew

of the nature of the sky
and the crushing of the heart
was the failure of place,
confusing two kinds of space:

where the beginning ends,
and where you see the beginnings
of your self being seen —
a difference that is the symptom

of time, in which
the arborescent book
is lost and lost,
and the city is never completely founded.

It is the same for us, half-dwellers,
reporting to the gods
that a fever might be frightened
or a swelling scared,

during the Paschal moon's increase,
for my vigour, my helmsman, my table,
provider of fuel to my broken rooms,
the one gazed upon in the morning.

## The Queen Maeve Bridge 1922-1942

In the limited light of the dawn
the sprightly owl observed the moon's
undulating sweeps on one decay path,
slowing down and speeding up by turns.

On cloudless atmospheric days
she could feel the iron sun
ruby-throating both sides of her tongue
like one fruit enclosed by another.

The icy worlds of faint galaxies
seemed to swarm in the spiral arms
of the Milky Way, deformed nestlings,
black and perfumed, with very beautiful veins.

Reins of ivy of a yellow pebble colour
showed her the rare earths
stolen as lightest elements by the stars,

how these are destroyed and contracted
deep inside them — the drag a star
experiences as it ploughs.

## Birds, Women and Writing

What was my last gift to you, this slack heart,
this white gaze? Tell me the first token,
brown berry or red river comb?

Do you remember that night on yon lean hill
when you and I were at the foot of the rowan
tree and the night was freezing?

We counted our days in nights, sorcerers, not
state animals. You twisted my tresses
to shoe my bare foot.

You made a pet out of a word-bird that landed
on your shoulder, a wasp-orchid, Irish-looking,
that flew out peacefully.

A higher wave erased it like a face drawn in sand
at the edge of the sea, and for a while
I no longer used the word,

even though I adore it. Where the corner of the room
curves down like a beak you came over to walk
between the open bay window,

your deepest step shaded like ovaries perhaps
against the heavens — as sometimes a child's presence
will happen only later.

Leave now those windows, and close my hands not resting
their blood-infused elbows reduced to write
*à l'eau rose.*

Songs whose story is elsewhere, passing through the opposite
of what is being approached, that
will not end sweetly.

The churchish skyline when it is almost snow-covered
will give the feeling of something being
taken away:

a woman-chair, whose song of rubbed thoraxes
calls to love, but makes the breath virginal
again. She does not like

to sing me the last verses, with their meagre
reassurance for suffering, no doubt accompanying us
the furthest along our way.

## Journey with S

We were spirit-calling
at an Irish house
with its thick masonry,
I, a hard sea-spirit,
you, a spirit of the cold.

I gave you my hair ornament:
you let it open and abrade
like the morning, soaked with prayer.

You said, he keeps her altar well
with the illness of the flowers
and the fevers of the little rocks,

and it seemed a birth chant
where each word should be seen
like an easy lotus on every side.

The widespread gates of her speech
melted into the familiar surroundings
of words, their indoor softness,

a pool of near daylight
where he woke from sleep to see
the source of his own blooming.

## My Love Has Fared Inland

Of December, the tenth day.
The shape of the hill,
the pent-up river,
the course of the stream,
parcelled out once more.

As he gradually
moved north that winter,
swathes in the grass
on two separate slopes
appeared to show the direction
in which that bloom
was already brushed aside.

The raw, scraped,
bludgeoned land
like a windmill
beneath a nutshell
tackled skies within
a paved parlour
and a groomed park

in what had seemed before
idyllic countryside.

## Emily Noether's Theorem

Poets are divided according to the rivers
that are closest to their home. He glances
at the lance in the lance-rack,
at his ago, the site of a single-hearth house,
which must come down in the bloomed fields,
thorns, earth, broom and overgrown grass.

Then pursues a heavy-heeled diagonal
towards Urania, robber of the verbal well,
with her purple riding scarf, saddle cloth
and cushion, seated next to Apollo,
who raises a lustrous quill,
conversing with that laureate whose signet finger
carved his own name in large letters
over the very breast of the mother of God,
on the black sash of his Pièta's Madonna.

The flutist poses in stocks with a clock
holding the brass flower which Dante wore
dressed in darkest pink, late as the mulberry,
while Petrarch masked in a sad green,
as leaves should shelter fruit,
accompanies Sappho's stockings of straw,
garters of felt, amazing sky-blue gloves,
his bare-breasted muse of choice,
brave in the next-to-nothing of a line.

## To my Daughter, Finding her Weeping,
## because I would not Consent to her Fasting

Twelve nights before midsummer
we thought we had been born too late.
They were no longer selling angels
but selling silence — I pushed against
the silence a bit further, my drive
into solitude cutting off those avenues
at the gothic bend of the street.

When I was struck by lightning
they covered me with earth.
My mouth covered half my face
like someone who has never lied.
My body was without a single great
circle, dangerously detached from its
core self, shod in its pilgrim role.

Only the stone threshold had been saved
from the ruins, in a landscape exposed
to different nuances, the reflection
of the stretching moon on navigable seas.
A lust image of sunset, which had lain
yellowing with the rest of the day's discharge,
turned its wirelike line of silver

in the solitary lines of my palms
where I dreamt about myself and my reproduction;
a silvery distorted red as long
as my gypsy table, a bridal pink and silver
on the open leaf of the bureau and my gossip
chair, in a parlour eight by eight
lit by three tallow candles.

All my weariness of the north
revived with double force, as the olive green
chrysoberyl reddens in lamplight. My pen
was encircled with silk thread
from ivory-silk curtains in adorned
luminous rooms. I would hand it on
to the afterworld for what will be served at tea

when the brilliancy of the flower
would be darker, when the quite dark words
would go on holiday, not here, not now, not us,
never skulking like other thrushes,
black wedge on more pointing wingtips,
angel with ankle boots . . .

They talk about their roofs and doors
but never darken these doors with their
mosaic of withdrawn hues, pearls buoyant
and heavy from municipal pawnshops.
For the first two minutes of the four minute
dance she does not move: he will bring a lily

who happened to come over from Corfu in his yacht.

## The Sulking Room

The blinds of scented grass embroidered
with the lighthouse of good omen
were dampened in heat — she would place five
red roses before her as she worked.

Doors must not be shut by her
nor cooking pots covered, nor the lids
of boxes let down: the dead brown petals
may never be swept out.

She may wear a marten around her neck
without any gold, her arm bare
of the marriage bracelet rotating like
a windmill becoming rosaries of quisqualis,

a tangle of white and pink, the bell-shaped
elephant creeper, with an extra knot
for the vow not revealed: seventy-two strands,
for the seventy-two names of the angels.

At second twilight she would hold
the lobes of her ears in crossed hands
and stand-sit without remission, not
to live in hell as a caterpillar,

or be exposed as an old sour plum-
tree to a swoop of birds. Everything
in the room fell in love with the death-
lamp alight, that made a spoon-shaped

group of stars image of her, the slave
of God's grammar, from the dust of her feet.

## Shelta

My run-a-gate of a grandfather,
clayer, one who manures or marls the land,
slept on some clover trusses
while frost covered one side of his body
with a fine childbed sheet.

I have directed his grave
to be covered with verdant turf,
where a robin with a white scar
on one of its wings, a simple, slow-moving bird,
is quietly pilfering.

The fields spread out in a wheel,
meadow eaten down by cattle,
bare ground beaten by the lambs
with their red necklaces in hot weather.
His eye would be drawn, passing over the garden,

to the yellow flowers of the leeks
grown in the threadbare thatch
as a charm against lightning —
to my red petticoat with its two gold laces,
to couch grass tangled in a plough.

A notice board sticks up
to all enquiring friends 'No Road Here',
written with bruised nut-galls, green copper, stone blue,
soaked in a pint and a half of rainwater, shaken every day,
with a small leaf from a tree of charity.

## The Poetry of Fire, Third Evening

Warmer to the fingers than to the lips,
why do you raise your arms instead
of clasping us in them? That timid
wintry pleasure clothing over the emotions
was a lesson in brilliance on the most complete
day of the year, mixing the seasons
together, with a sense of time drawing tight:
but there is no animal feeling in electricity.

Now in this infancy of the third millennium
often I think I could have been born farther east
where that severe climate that follows the artist,
white stitchwort, would run and run,
where that unknown clarity we discover
when everything is plundered, betrayed, sold,
stretches its white islandness
obliterating the stars.

Absurdly generous — rare as a box of flowers arriving
with all their heads cut off — he appears to be
drying dead champagne from a teacup, speaking
that voice you can say anything in
from garden to half-moon garden, those exquisite
borders within himself. She wears earrings of small
advent leaves, a fireside skirt of clearest yellow,
having a green lining sewn inches above the hem.

When the music strengthens, after its hesitation
cuts, and moves about as firelight might
or infectious laughter in a church, the heel
of her shoe snaps in two. By Women's Christmas,
a total death has left no trace,
the constant rain she was half-
hoping for, reaches into the neck
of her floral coat.

## The Muse of Electricity

I exist on a stony beach
which lowers itself in waves
towards a protective ocean.
Two mountainous shadows
loom over me, and where the shadows
are at their deepest, researching syllables,
I watch the light travel across
the space inside;

with straight light
the journey is brighter.
Doors and windows swap places,
the three walls that had their wallpaper
changed over and over
and the wallpaper-covered door
turn with quick, tinkling pulse beats
towards the dawn.

In the bright, unoccupied room,
tables have nothing
but an underside.
A table is laid
with a bowl of ice;
there is snow on the furniture.
A blush appears on my left palm
as someone walks across the intelligent island

like a nervous passenger asking
the sunken time. The little house
that had been built on
to the back of the house,
embedded like an anchor
at a greater depth,
violates the Coastal Act
with its pirated electricity, its piped Mozart.

At the high tidemark
the peculiar lemon desert fragrances
of two small yellow-brown patches
left decaying underneath
a summer cottage being restored
flatten out into blinding yellow
nightlights and car-oriented
twilights, nocturnal radiance.

Continual repair, gradual
piercing of the dark, until finally
a light shone
shiny as wine from just one window
of this strangely
unfinished house:
as if an ordinary person
has been lost in it,

quietly smoothing his bed,
as a harbour disappears
with the silting of the coast.
On land that has been mined
houses cave in, abysses open up,
streets rupture with a scented
warning, landscape quivering
with the coming of the spring.

When someone leaps
out of turbulent water, waving his arms,
leaving a perfectly smooth surface
behind him, a place
that was *there* changes into *here*,
less isolated, less complete,
a river taken on its own
whose name translates as 'out of the dark',

and will last only as long
as the rain. Any run
of warm days in the gateway
of September, after the first
frost, I would slip a good
twenty-five times out of my house
to walk around my future home
and count the footsteps I needed to do that,

without the intention of staying,
the faces by the wayside
like the many faces of a dead man.
Through flower and song I know
the difficulty of keeping watch.
As one second must be able
to stretch itself out, I will sit on a cliff,
looking out over the bay.

# Backwater with Beautiful Churches

During the past ten years,
getting it to make the right
sort of curve, all wanting-to-say
was de-cornered in a way.

Yet this message comes second,
crossing through danger and their
bleak steppes. He should have been
the first to say something, saying too much.

The language that held him ran
through him, a sea barely flushed,
suffocating itself into a trance,
kissing the planet goodbye.

The word has done a somersault
like the ambiguity of the jewel,
as if it had never lived on a body,
a point of light supporting our gaze.

How light's modesty is turned,
by a light-proof muzzle. How a beam
so pronounced like a milky cone
frosts the boughs in nickel and platinum.

Next to the eagerly expected
wood anemones, a silk bridge
of aluminium, a meandering
zinc stockade.

Even when the sky shows itself
in its qualities,
the scarred floor's
quota of sunlight,

apron of brocade, paisley
or willow, its almost minimal skin
is a virtual pathway
desertified, paved-over

wasteland actually seen,
by the eyelike container,
by the dark edge of bowl,
soft lead. The melted-down

statue reinstalled, apostle
to the apostles, where
the remains of the nine-thousand-
year-old fishing net were found.

# Yesterday's Bather

*for Sinéad Morrissey*

Imogen has put the book down
at this point, she takes a perfumed bath:
the wind, vision without eye,
smells her veins knotless as water
in the waves of peace.
It is no visual trespass,
the beach lays itself bare
in the form of a gentle shipwreck,
or the house turns its back to the sea
so the sea may be absent
and the view of the sea more precious
to lay the shipwreck to rest.

Tongues adorn the swanskin
of her shoulders with the right of flowing,
star kiss, marine kiss,
united by the red of her lips,
the moment of the hand lifted
to her lips or upon her shoulder,
the touch may go on swirling,
but are we so sure that his hand
will continue to rest there?
Eternal in the way that is possible
for it, these short weeks of eternity
that keep the world up like a bird in the air.

Sound of returning day-shy birds
with weaker tides, their sails drying
in the sun. A kind of dead rainbow
ribs the ceiling, within the walls
the hurrying net of two sisters.

But truly is she not like a cloud
in the threadbare heavens
that can slip into any shell at all,
ceaselessly outgrowing herself,
her eyes the hidden ostrich eggs
in thirsty garden mouths,
her knee-shaped canal a slender
collar of terra firma
for the marsh crocodile after the last bridge?

In her forehead are tied up
amber and a blade of straw.
She gave you her years, may you live.

## Child of the Wheel

Seeing it first from a doorway,
the eye of the house, usually facing
seawards, I call upon the image
of the calm abiding spirit owner
of a cliff not far from here.

To mark the field with border stones
was to balance autumn and spring:
though autumn wears a white prayer scarf
like spring's, but fastened at both shoulders,
whatever seasonal attribute she was holding,

the rake is missing. Thick reeds grow
above her head in the side fields.
No lotuses spread from her footprints,
no milk from her two fingers resting against
her cheek, to keep her body unchanging.

If I do not go there the soul-lake
where amazing omens of her death arose
does not produce any images — jewels inlaid
in its face, twelve ornaments at once,
like a person who has totally dissolved.

In this one-cornered cave of impermanence
with its many trees like a banquet display
or offering water, where the shovel
was never passed but rather replaced,
and the blade and the whetstone have disappeared,

this beggar, myself, could light a butter-lamp
to consult round mirrors in a rich cup
of acanthus roots, or lay a Tibetan carpet
over a Chinese sofa with not even attachment.

For the world is set by the speech of men,
far from the kitchen of the residence-hall
and the cross speech of the jealous kitchen-mistress.

# The Good Housewife

The good housewife should take care
that no part of the house, no place, no household goods
are hidden from her. She should look everywhere,
think of everything, go everywhere, so that
when she needs something she will have what she wants
under her eye, or under her hand, quickly
and without difficulty, like a captain who often
inspects his soldiers.

While she is sitting working, or doing some other duty
within her room, she should go over the whole house
in her mind, thinking whether there is anything lacking,
or anything in excess. All kinds of small and medium
yard animals should be fed at the right time.
She should know how to castrate cockerels,
and make sure that the bees are not attacked by pests.
Flax should be trampled on at night, and spinning
done in the stable. She should ensure that the front door
is safely locked, and the door which is halfway
up the stairs.

On Sundays she should make everyone change
into their white shirts. She should place herself
in the embrasures of windows so that she can have
enough light to do fine needlework and embroidery.
She should keep an eye on his wishes
as the helmsman, always steady and determined,
keeps his eye to the north.

About your pains, I ask you to think well
which disorder of food, air or clothes
could be the cause. In the meantime, and this
is the right season, get some wild rose-hips
which can be found on hedges. Now is the right time,
because the hedges have lost their leaves, and the rose-hips

are clearly visible, looking as if they are stuck
on top of little sticks. Better get those
from the hills than from the plains, because
they are more efficacious, not pale or black
ones, only nearly yellow ones that have been
more exposed to the sun.

Dry them in a shady place, and pound them
with some cinnamon. But do not eat pears,
just think about giving birth, and do not spend
such a long time reading that you will then do
everything else badly, first take care of everything else,
then you can read as much as you like.

## Shrive Gate

Rows of turf, eerily shielded from war,
the platform red with the spray of crocuses.
The last day was for the elephants —
elephant piety, elephant patriotism.

One elephant, whose feet were badly wounded,
crawled on its knees against the thrown spears;
entreating the crowd with gestures, it snatched
railings and hurled them into the air.

Take fresh brookwater, marking that the sun
does not shine thereon, and scatter some of its seed
back into the city as though it were my climate,
where the quayside cranes are dipped

like the soul across the body, the body's
nights, and chance leaves cover
the cloths tasselled at the corners
stretched too thinly. Berry Edge,

Apron and Blue. My room lay lying-in
between north and south, and was decisive
in my life, though it is always I who decide
that this voice is the voice of an angel,

or winds calling for soft scarves to be
pulled up. Bite the stem of flowers
for their leeless wine. Now you are the street,
speak in its name.

# The Girl who Turned into a Sunflower

Her Muse means water, the moisture on the banks,
which can be awakened by a drop of oil.
Her hair is bound by disturbing fidelity,
hands lingering around her neck
make her shoulder the shape of the island,
sprinkle a balsam that spasms the clouds.

He had won her in an archery contest,
a tame stag who wore pearl earrings
descended from a work of art, the head,
though not the body, painted from life.
Cries of animals hunted centuries earlier
took possession of the mountain.

Apples tended by nymphs of the evening
and effortlessly harvested had been the earth's
wedding present, the losers in the singing contest
mutated into magpies. She gave birth as a myrrh tree
narrated across forty-four north wall windows.
Were it not for her exhausted transformations

she would know the hedge behind the Muses
is of unchanging laurel and resists fire.

## The Ginger Jar

It is five miles to that familiar European-
English cloud that is trying to bring
the islands together, no simple matter.

Each ragged island from rim to rim
has the leftover shape of wreckage
behind spray; even under the nearest past

one seems to be heading northwest
like a halved lemon, a fat pen nib seen
at its most naked driving a snare of yellow

into a wedge of pure night. If we follow
the rippling fringe of the pale roads
we see no seated girls nursing guitars

as if they were babies, none playing Patience
looking at her own profile, her breasts'
little cages, a couple of apples that images

are being suspended in, but so unfree a colour,
most often in the outlines of petals, or overlapping
laurel leaves, that rhyming blue oval round

the edges of flowers, mild and ambiguous.
A lightweight colour — a lavender triangle trapped
by squares of luminous scarlet in the brightest

strata of the sky, where the only meaning
in his repertoire of touches is that he has
sometimes said that he 'likes trees'.

## Desh: The Homeland

They have arranged for me to visit the house
in their own dedicated region, an innocent bystander.
Behind the windows it is only marginally warmer
and certainly darker than outside — a mush
of grey and green remains in my mind.
It is a small space, easy to commit to memory,
and easy to play with in one's imagination.
Mentally, I rearrange the furniture, re-light
the room and heat it up. I sit long enough
to imagine their movements on this confined
stage (trust Shakespeare to have been there before)
and conclude that no amount of re-decoration
will turn it into the comfortable salon they deserved.
It is a lesson in modesty — under these tightly
curled stairs they took their meals crushed
by the news of assassinations, or menaced
from within, and no kindness when kindness was due.

From the house of the living I may as well go
to the house of the dead. Gates surround the churchyard,
but they are wide open, there is no cemetery
to speak of, only the character, the mood
of an incorrect city — shrubs and grass and moss
and muddy lanes amid the tall trees. I find
the grave much where I thought it would be,
in the back part, behind the new church,
to the south and east, a vertical tombstone,
unweathered and unadorned, blue and edgy,
its blank page blanching the skin. But how strong,
how precise, how ample! Making wishes more clear
now, what we cry for, across a lifetime.
Besides announcing whose grave it is, that naked
and proper word, the inscription reads 'Caute',
which is Latin for 'Be Careful', printed just beneath
the drawing of a rose.

The startle reflex in the theatre of my body
closes the locks for fear and anger on the maps
of sorrow . . . I look at the child with his long eyebrows
resting on the wing of a swan, where the flags have taken
wing to a brittle star like Sedna, and am reminded
of Descartes' 'He who hid well lived well'.
As I leave my thoughts turn to the bizarre
significance of this burial site — how fitting it all
is, Bento, Baruch, Benedictus, blessed,
all that gossip from deep within the deepest rhymes
and reasons. And without that once, my ever since
feelings are, the quietly hidden insula
may be the most important of all.

## South of Mars

It's over now. Part of the story
has disappeared, into the void
of something that has ended forever:
I know the exact place, behind the house,
a place where waves can be counted,
seven hard cold waves,
like the ones in the sea.

Undreamt of blues and marvellous
greys set up a background,
a flat light and a mask of ocean salt,
for a sea full of inlets, harbours
and ravines, shipwrecks and sudden
green splendours: green, I want you,
green, I am half-full of seawater

though far, far from the sea,
and the smoothest stone
is a freshwater myth.
A cool oval breeze reaches me
from the sea, birds can fly in it,
and every half-minute comes the smell
of the sea, newly cleaned, like a loaf of silver.

The sound of the sea fits inside
an orange in a wicker basket,
or your face when it is still wet.
Its fine sand, of which there is very little,
licks the shell of the sunset without
waiting to go in, as if I had
a gold coin in my hand and didn't

know how to let it go.
I'll do the whole thing in one breath,
and soon this house will be happier

and more logical, without the dark
corridor, without its quiet humble plume
of smoke that was warm blood
mistaken inside a windowpane.

When you're all in the door of your house
with that sense of Saturday and garden gate
you'll know there's no place I'd rather live
to finish out the summer, the last days of August
and the blessed September,
above all, waking up,
and finding *that*.

Send me news how the sea is doing,
wave-like wheat and wheat-like wave.
Remember me when you
are at the beach, in that yacht
with the name of an island —
I would like the water to grow calm
for you and send blue telegrams.

My back to the frozen field
and just one star, I have the joy
of thinking very differently than I did
last summer, the year that the pillow
was embroidered. Who would have said
that eight years later I would look
for the timid city on the map

to see the mountain stripped of mist
and *not* look at the sea,
the church tower rock back and forth
over the pitiable houses? A verbal
and musical ruin. I never understood

the number in your address this past
season, your passport of smiles

like a train without wheels
or wheels without a track.
Surrounded by corpulent trees,
as if the tree had just been invented,
the woman who went to gather kindling
on the beach of day sits down
with all the excitement produced by jewels.

But anything is better than to remain
seated in the window looking
at the same landscape and its surprises.
The sadness that slackens electrical lines
can lengthen the radio waves
of its golden poverty. Perhaps
what we thought would cast a thick shadow

will cast none at all. And thirty Aprils
traced by your fingers will sit down
in the shadowless nudity
of the last lamps, letting the things
themselves decide where their shadows
fall, the cool shadow of that blood,
watching all things take flight.

## A New Portrait in the Naughton Gallery

About the distance you'd stand from someone,
like a whispered secret that goes around a room,
it was centred on its wall, where daylight would fall,
later on in the year, after this tangible season.

I wanted to step forward and warm my hands on it:
it had something to do with the war, the charred,
burnt-up books — it had lovely air — it smelled
as if it were scented with the finest particles

of disintegrated books — it held me in thrall.
It was like peering between the shelves
of a library, beyond a wall of books,
coloured an impossibly smooth and chilling blue,

which made the picture easier to see.
How icy, its petrified quiet! I measured
its shadows with my eyes. The light
was so low and siccative, like flour

settling into a sieve, at the lip
of an abyss. The painting would not say
in its alpine lateness if it was lonely,
or if, clearly, it is time to go.

My eye was rebuffed by the dim canvas —
how beautiful, how flat! It was sealed
off from me like a relic, a prize antique
in a funeral parlour, but the hand

that does not reach out on to our side
of the painting was trying to gather
me in, like a wound fading back
into perfect skin. It is not sounds

that have to be subtracted, the city noises
hush. You stare into a deep chasm,
an ageing thinning with no floor
where everything is partly sacred

because nothing is quite what it should be.
It looks still and quiet, it runs from hot to cold,
and the young man of thirty years is drained out
by a cloudburst at the upper left hand corner

whose wine trembles as he holds it still.
Rain comes from great distances, where things
were ill seen and ill said
and every beam of light comes in

a high window, and strikes a dusty bookcase.
It is dully painted,
but there are eight brilliant reflections
in peeling bronze along the top edge

that the lamp must house, imperceptibly
tipping the balance of the colour towards blue.
He is dressed in monk's robes, looking up
into the sky, surrounded by a bluish sea

chalky and dry, as if he were a boulder
in a stream, or melting into a cliff.
Some of the books are safety-glass blue,
or bottle-blue, or the blue of cold, wet grass

which darkens downwards towards his feet,
though above his head they are creamy,
perhaps reflecting the afternoon sun.
As you glance below the cream dies

to a fluorescent beige, then chafes
to a torn turquoise, as if he were wading
in a chlorinated pool, moving slowly
in the direction of the deep end.

There is no green, though some of the blues
are stained by browns and scatters of dirt,
a fuzz of blighted thorns.
The ripped surface reflects no tender

sap, but a wan or toxic fog,
the slate-grey of a close-cropped field,
parched and marred by thistles.
Is he looking up at the sun?

Possibly — for he has a tiny yellow
glint in his eye, as if someone has just
jumped into it. It is only night time
in the plunging front of the portrait,

but it is not in some faraway place:
it seems to grow older
along with me, as it sinks
forever into the way I think.

## Nil Mansions

Cargo 200. A white accident, a stroke
of the body called the field
on itself from within its equator:
even the mountains look unkempt and shabby,
without earth in his mouth.

The fever crystallized, breathing from somewhere
under his body, like a new muslin richly spangled,
elf-shot: the collar was supposed
to tighten around his neck
if ever he gave a false judgement.

From my seat in the upper deck of the outfield
a timber track turns me to the wave
of the world, down to blossoming Milan;
the rake of the house is steep, the maps
on their silver panels are only 'sort of' open.

Did my folder of notes stay closed? The sight
of his bold, black, looped writing
in the desert of my own excites me like
treasure-trove. The brooch, however,
is over a thousand years younger,

as if it were not our lucre
that erected his sanctuary.
Everything he saw had the look things have
when a band is passing. But our words
and your glances no longer form an angle,

those eye-splitting words, the saccades
of the eye, facing a choice between two
glances. Time must be whiled
until you feel strong enough
to gaze out of the window:

you did not press that last metabreath
out of yourself, roughly wasting breath
so carefully stored. A new phrasing
of breath as the next ghost rises, and
for good or ill he will not lightly leave.

You are closer to winter, the lights come up
faster tonight and, see, I have brought you
a small bottle of scent entitled
'Ce Soir ou Jamais'. An alluring book
urging us to shipwreck.

I know when he opens his eyes, and when
he smiles, when he moves his other worldly
force — if you give up your moments
before they are full, lips may approach
only after losing.

A curve in the stage's lip
in which fields come to be:
I have changed — will you answer
in time? Once a circle closes
there is no return.

You are crossing the circle, or have
passed through the false depth
of its centre: is too much
of the circle behind you
to take the last train home?

## Tertulia

Curious little train: I picture you
helmeted and bucklered, in recoil
to the black swelling of the north names,
the same shallow white beds of turnips.

Visitors found the only city I have ever
been grateful to, half dead, subdued
and dying, its modest bread-girls
picking rags with ramshackle harpoons,

its joy-worn flags looped up by one corner.
In a chunk of streetlight, under the useless
lash of a tree, the dewy lip of one of the sugar
tables is banded round by keen shadows.

A word you are hearing a dozen times
a week — a proto-keyword whose meaning
seems exhausted by the nine-armed cyclist
police, their way of courting early

images within the late ones. But this
to excavate the deepest possible
well of violet autumn air,
even when there isn't any of it.

## Yellow Ultramarine

Wood cut in autumn is denser
than wood in spring;
the exceptionally poisonous and treacherous
emerald green
will drown in gold the much-praised earth.

Like safely burnt light
the unbleached leaf
lies over the ground like a veil,
to be pulled completely off like a skin.
Its turning grey is a poor-looking colour

with a piercing odour.
But equally white, the old parts
have grown through this retarded drying.
Their mysterious yellows
re-carve the west wind's original spiral position

in relation to the core of the tree.
The glass in a picture frame
that seeks brightness above everything
can come too close to the canvas pores.
And if the canvas is held

to the sensitive middle ear
the sweetness of the colour will return,
as if all the colour needed
were the Naples yellow
roasted on to the tiles of Babylon.

The author acknowledges the financial support of the Arts Council of Northern Ireland while she was writing these poems.